Faux Florals

IN GLASS

Thanks to the following people and companies for their assistance and products: John S. Maciejny; Koehler & Dramm Wholesale Florist, Minneapolis, Minnesota; Smithers-Oasis; LaLa Imports, El Paso, Texas; Teters Floral Products, Inc., Bolivar, Missouri.

acknowledgments

Creative Publishing international

First published in the United States of America by Creative Publishing international, Inc., a member of Quayside Publishing Group
400 First Avenue North
Suite 300
Minneapolis, MN 55401
1-800-328-3895
www.creativepub.com

ISBN-13: 978-1-58923-423-9
ISBN-10: 1-58923-423-5

Library of Congress Cataloging-in-Publication Data
Beveridge, Ardith.
  Faux florals in glass : 30-plus unique arrangements in clear vases and other glassware / Ardith Beveridge.
    p. cm.
  Includes index.
  ISBN 1-58923-423-5
  1. Flower arrangement. 2. Artificial flowers. I. Title.
  SB449.3.A7B48 2008
  745.92--dc22
                                            2008008316
                                                 CIP

Copy Editor: Catherine Broberg
Proofreader: Ron Hampton
Book Design and Page Layout: Dawn DeVries Sokol
Cover Design: Dawn DeVries Sokol

Printed in the USA

Faux Florals
IN GLASS

30-plus
Unique Arrangements
in Clear Vases and
Other Glassware

Ardith Beveridge

Creative Publishing
international

contents

designs for special events ... 104

designing with *glass* containers

As you roam the aisles of your favorite craft or home décor store, you'll find hundreds of clear and colored glass containers, from basic vases to ornate sculptural pieces. It's obvious that many of these containers are intended to hold flowers—fresh or faux—but others were designed to be something else, such as serving pieces, storage canisters, or candle holders. I'd like you to also see glass containers as the starting point for long-lasting, décor-boosting floral arrangements made with permanent botanicals, popularly known as faux or silk flowers.

Creating faux floral designs in glass containers poses a few challenges because you can't hide the mechanics of the design down in the container or buried in ordinary floral foam. On the bright side, glass containers offer lots of possibilities for creativity in your designs. What shows through the glass is both decorative and functional. I'll show you how to overcome the challenges and use the clear properties of glass containers to show off permanent botanicals in beautiful, innovative ways.

Today's permanent botanicals look so real, you have to touch them to know the difference. Their wired stems, also realistic, are easy to manipulate and will hold the shape you give them. Sometimes you may choose to design the florals outside or on top of the container. There are no limits. This book will show you how, and before you know it, you'll be looking at those glass containers with an entirely new vision.

Here are thirty original floral designs in glass containers of all different shapes and sizes. All the materials and tools you'll need are available in hobby and craft stores. Some specialty items can be ordered through your local florist. You'll find these same glass containers and lots of similar ones in craft stores, home décor stores, gift shops, and florist shops. You may even have some on your shelves at home. Each project includes a materials list and step-by-step instructions with lots of photographs. If you love every aspect of the design and want to create it exactly as pictured, simply follow my directions. If you have difficulty finding a particular floral material, feel free to substitute something with similar color, shape, and texture, using the photographs on pages 13 and 14 as a guide. If the shape and style are right but you need a different color, simply choose similar flowers in your own color scheme, using the information on color (pages 10 to 12) to help you.

Before you begin, please read through the first section. You'll find valuable information on materials and techniques—the same information that I include when I teach floral design classes to crafters and budding professionals. Then choose an interesting glass container for your first project and get creative!

Always, Ardith

techniques *and design*

floral design *basics*

Whenever you choose a project from this book, start by thinking about where you plan to display the finished design. A floral arrangement can brighten any area, from the entryway to the bathroom vanity, and can sit at any height, from the floor to an overhead ledge.

Location affects many aspects of good floral design. For example, it determines the angles from which the design will be seen. A centerpiece has to look good from every seat at the table. In fact, many table arrangements are seen from the sides as well as the front. On the other hand, a vase on an entry table will probably not be seen from the back—unless, of course, it's in front of a mirror! An arrangement on a low coffee table will be seen from above. You want to pick a design that will look good from all the visible sides.

Location also affects how big the arrangement should be. Do you want a focal point for the room, or an accent? The design should fit the available space around and above it without being intrusive and should be similar in scale to the rest of the room's furnishings.

If people will walk closely by the arrangement, the flowers can't stick out. This becomes a consideration with table designs that are placed in halls and entrances. Also consider whether the design will be in a formal or quiet space or where children will be playing.

Will the arrangement be seasonal or year-round? Many people enjoy changing their faux florals with the seasons, mirroring the flowers that would be growing during that time. However, you may want to create something that will look appropriate

longer. Some designs can be altered to extend their life by switching some or all of the flowers or adding accents associated with the season.

choosing and combining colors

Color is the most important element of any floral design. After all, color is what flowers are all about. When you look at the design above, the first thing you see is orange! Also, more than any other element of a design, color interacts with the surroundings. Because every flower does not come in every color, your choices are limited to what is available. Yet there are endless ways to combine colors, and experimenting with color is lots of fun. Here are some insights that will help you choose and combine colors effectively.

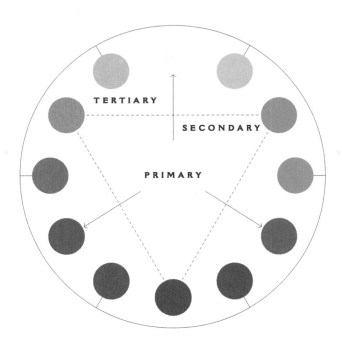

a

First, floral designs usually look best when one color dominates and the other colors support it. A rule of thumb is to use two-thirds of the dominant color, a quarter of the second color, and about a tenth of an accent color. Dark, intense colors usually work best in the center or base of the design, with light colors toward the edges. However, you may want to mix a few darker flowers near the outside of the design and a few lighter colors near the center to help it all balance.

Warm colors (red, orange, yellow) tend to dominate other colors and may seem to project out from the design. Cool colors (green, blue, and violet) are calm and restful. They tend to blend into the background of a floral design.

Consider the ways the room's lighting will affect the colors. In dim light, colors look muted. The yellow glow of candlelight and incandescent lighting can turn pink to peach and baby blue to gray. Cool colors and blends tend to fade away in dim light.

Floral designers, like other artists, use the color wheel to show the relationship between colors and to help them choose colors that will work well together. On a color wheel, the twelve basic colors are arranged by how they are created and how they relate to each other.

Red, yellow, and blue are called primary colors as they are not made from other colors. Orange, green, and violet are called secondary colors. Each is made by combining equal amounts of primary colors. Red plus yellow equals orange. Yellow plus blue equals green. Blue plus red equals violet. The two-name colors (red-orange, blue-violet) are called tertiary. They are made by combining one primary color and one secondary color in equal or unequal amounts.

The color wheel can help you anticipate how certain combinations of colors will look in a floral design. Here are some possible color schemes for floral designs.

a. Monochromatic: This is a design in one color. The design will be more interesting if the color is used in various intensities. In the example above, pale green glads are accented with green echinacea heads. In monochromatic arrangements, textures become more important.

b

c

b. Analogous: An analogous design uses colors that are next to each other on the color wheel. For example, the design above uses various shades of yellow, yellow-orange, and orange.

c. Complementary: This scheme uses florals in colors located on opposite sides of the color wheel—for example, bright red anthuriums stand out against green sago palm leaves. The design will have strong contrast.

d. Triadic: This scheme uses colors that are the same distance apart on the color wheel. When used correctly, a triadic design can be rich and dramatic. The peach and violet flowers and dark green foliage, used in the arrangement at right, form a triadic color scheme.

d

the florals

The projects in this book use faux flowers, which are available in many forms in craft stores and floral design centers. The following information will help you select and work with these materials.

permanent botanicals

Today's faux floral products are often so realistic that it's difficult to tell that they are not real. In the floral industry, faux florals are properly called "permanent botanicals." However, they are commonly referred to as "silk flowers," even though most are not made of silk but rather of polyester, latex, plastic, or a combination of materials.

Faux florals can be purchased in a wide range of qualities and prices, from inexpensive stems in solid colors to realistic stems with shading and veining. Most are made by machine. Hand-wrapped florals, at the higher end, are assembled by hand, though the parts may be made by machine. They may be parchment or fabric and are very realistic with wired stems and leaves. Some parchment and fabric flowers are dipped in latex to make them look more natural. "Dried silk" flowers have a crinkled appearance with curled edges and resemble real dried flowers.

Faux florals are produced in four standard forms: the bush, the fantasy flower, botanical-like, and botanically correct.

Bush. A bush is a group of flowers and foliage on one stem, perhaps including accent flowers. A bush may include one type of flower or a combination. It is reasonably priced and easy to use whole or cut into individual stems.

Fantasy flowers. These flowers resemble real flowers but have been designed to look different. For example, a flower might be made in a color in which it would not naturally exist, so that it can be used in a design where that color is needed.

Botanical-like. The florals are closer to the real thing, but the color, stem, foliage, or petal pattern has been changed to suit the desires of consumers. For example, a rose bush might have baby-blue flowers and have no dying flowers or broken stems.

Botanically correct. These are as close as possible to the real thing, though, of course, without the fragrance. The stem, pollen, leaf, root system, color, and branching structure are copied directly from nature. There is a remarkable degree of realism. Today's botanically correct florals look, feel, and are as flexible as real flowers. You may need to touch them to prove they are not fresh.

While botanically correct flowers and many botanical-like flowers are not inexpensive, they can be used as the focal point of an arrangement that includes inexpensive accent flowers. Top-quality florals are long lasting, so when you are tired of their first use, you can clean them and use them in other arrangements for added value.

flower roles

Flowers play certain roles in an arrangement, based on their shapes and sizes. If you can't find a particular flower, but you know its role, you can substitute something similar.

1. Line flowers. Shaped like a spike or having a long stem, a line flower establishes the height and width of the arrangement. Examples are gladiolus, larkspur, snapdragon, and liatris.

3. Form flowers. A form flower has a distinctive shape that attracts the eye and gives interesting visual texture to the arrangement. Examples are lilies, callas, orchids, anthuriums, and irises.

2. Mass flowers. A mass flower is a single, large, round flower that adds bulk and texture to a design. Examples are peonies, hydrangea, carnations, and pincushion protea.

4. Accent flowers. Also called "filler flowers," they accent the spaces between the main flowers and are usually added last. They include gypsophila, caspia, statice, and wax flower.

Note how the flowers in this
arrangement play different roles.

glass *containers*

Clear and colored glass containers are everywhere. While not all of them were created to hold flowers, with a little imagination, most of them can. Many of the containers used for the projects in this book are readily available at stores that carry floral craft supplies. Some of the designs are created in household items like pitchers or bottles. If you can't find the exact container, you're likely to find something similar that will work just as well. The main factors to consider are the size and shape of the container and the size of the opening.

Also consider how the container is weighted. Is the base heavy enough to keep the container from tipping? This is especially important for designs that are created mostly at the top of the container. Of course, you can always add decorative materials to the container, such as glass marbles or beads, stones, sand, or dried legumes to add weight to the base.

For some of the designs in this book, floral foam is secured to the bottom of the container. Rather than gluing the foam directly to the glass, first apply a strip of aisle tape, which looks like white duct tape. Then glue an anchor pin to the tape and secure the foam to the anchor pin. When you want to reuse the container, simply peel off the tape.

I like to be able to reuse my containers, which is one of the reasons I have not used artificial water in any of the projects. While glass is the perfect material for this product, remember it is a permanent, one-time use. Once the product has been poured into the container, it can't be removed.

If you do want your floral arrangement to look like it is in water, I recommend just using water. Most permanent botanicals are not harmed by water. Of course, as water evaporates, it leaves a ring of mineral deposits on the glass, so it isn't a good idea to leave the water in the container for more than a day at a time. For a special occasion, though, this can be very effective, especially if you also drop in submersible, battery-operated lights. Instant drama! When you want to reuse the container and the flowers, just empty the water and let the flowers dry.

cleaning glass

One of the challenges in working with glass containers is getting them sparkling clean—free of smudges, fingerprints, and mineral deposits. There are several good ways to keep your glass containers clean and shiny.

Do

- Before washing, wipe the vase inside and out to remove any dust.
- Wash in warm, sudsy water using mild, unscented dish soap. Clean the glass with your fingers or a new sponge. An old sponge may have residue from the last cleaning.
- Rinse with hot water, dry immediately with a soft, clean, dry towel. When the cloth becomes damp, change to a fresh one to prevent streaking.
- Try drying glass with black-and-white newspapers or a coffee filter.
- If the vase looks foggy, soak it in white vinegar for a few hours; then wash as above.

- To clean hard water deposits, use a mixture of vinegar and water, and scrub with a bottle brush. If the neck is too small for a brush, pour the solution into the container, add some uncooked rice, and shake.
- For heavy buildup, fill the container with water and dissolve a denture cleaner tablet. Let it sit; then empty and rinse.
- Use rubbing alcohol to remove sticky substances like hair spray.

Do not
- Clean vases in direct sunlight or wind because the cleaning solution will dry before you can wipe it clean.
- Use detergent. It will leave a film on the glass.
- Use the dishwasher. It might chip the glass.
- Use steel wool pads. They will scratch the glass.

To ensure long life for your glass containers, take care when handling and storing them. Always carry glass containers with both hands, one at the base and one at the top. Glass rims and stems can be very delicate. Never pick up a vase by its rim; never hold a container by the stem while washing or drying it. Be sure to clean glass thoroughly before storing it. To protect the rim, always store containers standing up. Make sure they have a little breathing room so containers don't bump each other on a shelf or in a cupboard.

materials *and tools*

You will want to set up a design space with tools and materials readily at hand. Tools and materials for creating beautiful floral arrangements are available in craft stores, from florists, and wherever quality faux flowers are sold.

anchoring materials

1. Styrofoam is sold in white, greens, and browns in various sizes and shapes. It is used for anchoring thick-stemmed faux florals and materials on picks. When cutting Styrofoam with a knife, run the sharp blade edge into the side of an old candle or a bar of hand soap before each cut, to help the knife cut smoothly and make less noise.

2. Dried floral foam is sold in blocks and sheets, available in greens, browns, and bright colors. It grips stems securely and will not melt when glue or paint is applied. Rainbow foam (as shown on pages 120 and 121) also comes in powdered form and can be used with either permanent or fresh flowers.

3. Container weights. Marbles, sea glass, stones, and glass beads, in a variety of colors, sizes, and shapes, are used to add physical and visual weight to the design, especially apparent when designing with glass containers.

4. Anchor pins. Small plastic circles with prongs. The circle is secured to the bottom of a container and the prongs hold floral foam in place.

adhesives and securing materials

5. Glue pan. A small electric skillet used to melt glue pellets.

6. Pan glue pellets. Nuggets or blocks of adhesive melted in a glue pan. Don't mix with glue sticks. Do not mix glues from different companies, as the chemical composition is different and the mixture may not adhere.

7. Paintbrush and honeystick. An inexpensive 2" (5 cm) paintbrush or a honeystick (page 22) used to apply glue to items too large or awkward to dip in the pan.

8. Small clay saucer. Placed in the glue pan to keep the brush and honeystick from resting on the bottom of the pan where they could burn.

9. Duct tape. One sided, all-purpose tape, 2" (5 cm) wide, with a silver-gray surface. Available in white, called aisle runner type. Used to attach foam temporarily.

10. Anchor tape. Narrow tape on a roll in green, white, or clear; ½" (1.3 cm) width for large projects and ¼" (6 mm) width for small designs. Used for securing foam to the vessel.

11. Glue gun. Hot-glue tool used to secure foam and add trims. The high-temperature variety is best for faux floral work.

12. Glue sticks. For the glue gun; in white, clear, and glittered. This glue does not hold in cold temperatures, so don't use it on outdoor holiday designs. Choose the type recommended by the manufacturer of your glue gun.

13. Floral tape. Self-sealing, wrapping tape in greens, browns, white, and rainbow colors. Used in floral design to wrap wires and lengthen stems.

14. Double-sided tape. Tape with adhesive on both sides; resists moisture and temperature extremes. Used for securing foam, candles, and accessory items like sea shells.

15. Wood picks. Thin pieces of wood with a point on one end and a thin wire on the other, in green, brown, and natural. Used to secure objects like artificial fruit, to stabilize tall designs, and to extend stems. The 6" and 9" (15.2 and 22.9 cm) lengths will fill most of your needs.

16. Floral wire. Used to bind floral materials together and to lengthen stems that are too short for the design. Wires are 18" (45.7 cm) long and are sized in gauges from 16 to 28; the smaller the number, the thicker the wire. Wire in 24-gauge is versatile for faux floral designs.

Glue dots (not shown). Small round discs of clear adhesive that come on a paper backing. Simply peel them off and use them as needed.

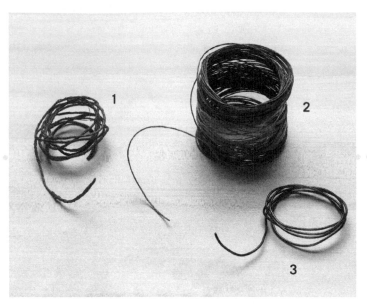

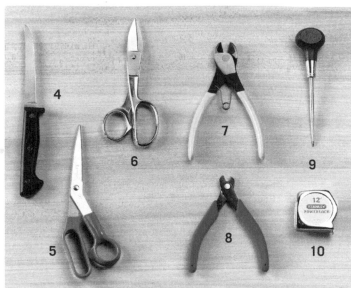

specialty wires

1. Barked wire is a heavy-gauge wire that is wrapped with brown or green raffia to look like a natural vine. It is used for supporting structures and binding heavy items to a base.

2. Bindwire comes in a roll in natural and green colors. It is 26-gauge wire covered with raffia to blend into your designs. Leave the outer plastic band on the roll and pull the wire from the inside to prevent the bindwire from becoming tangled. (Read manufacturer's directions.)

3. Aluminum craft wire comes in several colors. Though relatively thick, it is very pliable and will hold the shape you give it. When designing with glass containers, aluminum wire is useful for anchoring stems as well as for decorative effects.

tools

4. Knife. Large, sharp knife for cutting foam and a smaller sharp knife for shaping foam. Choose a knife that feels comfortable in your hand. Sharpen after each use, and keep in a toolbox or other safe place.

5. Scissors. For cutting ribbon, foliage, fabrics, paper, or other items that do not contain metal. Sharpen regularly.

6. Shears. Very useful tool for cutting small wires and wired ribbon. Does not need to be sharpened.

7. Wire cutters. For cutting faux floral stems. Blades are shaped for cutting close to the stem.

8. Utility snips. For cutting thick stems, branches, and thick wire.

9. Awl. Sharp pointed metal rod for poking holes in firm materials.

10. Tape measure. For measuring foam size, stem lengths, and design proportions.

floral *techniques*

Frequently used methods are explained here in more detail. Follow these techniques to complete your projects more efficiently and professionally.

preparing florals

When you buy a faux flower, it has been traveling a long way in a small box packed tightly with lots of other florals. So before you put it into a design, you need to fluff every flower and leaf. Bend and shape the stem. Open up the flowers and arrange the leaves in a natural way.

Many floral materials also need to be reinforced so the flower heads won't separate from the stems later. This is particularly true when the head and leaves have been made separately and slipped over the stem. Check the flower parts. If they aren't securely fastened, remove those parts. Then apply glue to the peg on the stem and reposition the leaf or flowers. Allow the glue to dry before you work with the material.

cutting stems

Always cut a floral stem at a sharp angle. The point makes it easier to insert the stem into foam. Cut floral stems with a wire cutter. Often a faux floral stem includes several flowers as well as foliage. The instructions may say to cut the stem into pieces. Find a section in the main stem that has a long distance between smaller branches. Cut the main stem at an angle just above the lower branch, as in the photo at right. This will give the upper stem the length it needs. The flower at the end of the lower stem will top the newly cut stem.

If it is necessary to disguise the cut, touch up the area with paint to match the stem color. Often leaves can be bent or turned to hide a cut.

lengthening a stem

At times you will need to lengthen a stem so it will work in your design. Perhaps you've cut a stem apart into pieces and some of the pieces just aren't long enough. You can easily extend a stem with wire.

1. Cut a floral wire as long as the present stem plus the length you want the stem to be extended. Hold the wire alongside the faux floral stem.

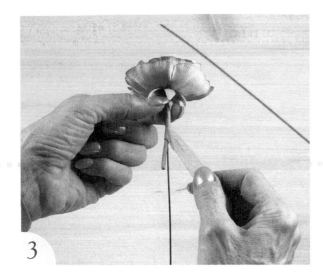

3

2. Wrap floral tape around the calyx (base of the blossom), gently stretching the tape and pressing the tape onto itself. Floral tape is a reversible strip of crepe paper coated with wax on either side. As the tape stretches, the wax is released to secure the floral tape to the stem. The warmth of your fingers softens the wax, causing the tape to stick to itself.

3. Twirl the floral stem with one hand, so the tape spirals around and down the stem, covering the stem and wire together. Stretch and warm the tape between the thumb and index finger of your other hand. The tape should overlap slightly with each wrap and leave no gaps. However, too much tape will give a bulky, unnatural appearance.

4. When you run out of floral stem, continue wrapping to the bottom of the wire. Then tear the tape from the roll (it is not necessary to cut it). Seal the end of the tape to the end of the wire by rolling the stem in your fingers.

wrapping floral wire

Floral wire is often wrapped with tape to make it easier to handle and less visible in the design.

1. Hold the end of the tape at the top of the wire. Twirl the wire in one hand while you wrap it with tape in spirals moving down the wire. Overlap the tape slightly and leave no gaps.

2. At the bottom of the wire, tear the tape. Seal the tape to the end of the wire by rolling the wire between your fingers.

using a glue pan

A glue pan works at a lower and more variable temperature than a glue gun. Place the pan on a piece of hard plastic or ceramic tile to protect your design surface. When you turn off the glue pan, you can keep the glue in it until next time. Set the temperature so that the glue is liquid but not smoking. There are two ways to apply the glue to materials.

Dipping. Floral foam and faux floral stems can be dipped into the glue pan before you secure them.

Brushing. When an object is too large or awkward to dip, you can transfer glue from the pan with a 2" (5 cm) paintbrush or a homemade honeystick. To make a honeystick, wrap a 12" (30.5 cm) chenille stem or pipe cleaner (one without metallics) around 2" (5 cm) at the end of a 9" (22.9 cm) wood pick or any strong natural wood stick or branch (nothing plastic, cloth, or metal).

using a glue gun

A glue gun is the best way to apply glue directly to a design—for example, to attach flowers or add trim. Heat the gun, place the tip where you want the glue, pull the trigger, and move the gun in a circular motion ending with an upward movement to break off the glue. The glue will be hot; if you aren't careful, you can get a nasty burn. Also, when the glue is hot, it will ooze out of the gun end at a touch of the trigger, so please be careful. Rest the gun on a stone tile or other nonflammable surface.

making a bow

You can add a bow to any floral design to give it added color or to make it a gift. Many ribbons are one-sided. The following method for making a loop bow keeps the decorative (right) side of the ribbon facing outward and the matte side hidden inside the loops.

1. Cut a 24-gauge wire in half and set it aside on the work table. Unroll about a yard (meter) of 1" (2.5 cm)-wide ribbon, but don't cut it. Grasp the ribbon between your left thumb and index finger, with the right side (shiny side) of the ribbon facing up; leave a tail of the desired length below your hand.

2. Make a sharp half-twist in the ribbon at the point where you are grasping it, and hold the twist between your thumb and finger; the matte side of the ribbon will now be facing up above your hand.

3. Bring the ribbon down over your thumb in a small loop, wrapping the ribbon flat against the twist on the underside; slip it between your thumb and finger. The matte side will again be facing up above your hand.

4. Make a sharp half-twist in the ribbon again at the point where you are grasping it, and hold the twist between your thumb and finger. The right side of the ribbon will now be facing up above your hand.

5. Turn under the ribbon, forming a loop above your hand and bringing the matte side of the ribbon flat against the twists on the underside. Slip the ribbon between your thumb and finger. The matte side of the ribbon will now be facing up below your hand.

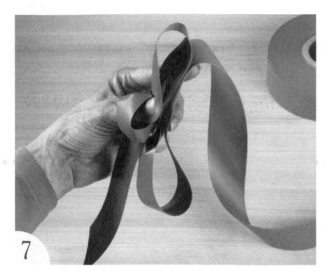

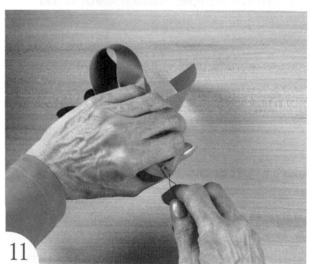

6. Make a sharp half-twist in the ribbon again at the point where you are grasping it, and hold the twist between your thumb and finger. The right side of the ribbon will now be facing up below your hand.

7. Turn under the ribbon, forming an equal loop below your hand, bringing the matte side of the ribbon flat against the twists on the underside; slip it between your thumb and finger. The matte side will now be facing up above your hand.

8. Repeat steps 4 to 7 at least twice or until you have made the desired number of loops. Make each pair of loops the same size or slightly larger than the pair above them.

9. Give the ribbon a final half-twist and slip the twist between your finger and thumb with the other twists. Cut the ribbon at an angle, leaving a tail of the desired length.

10. Insert a wire through the thumb loop so the middle of the wire rests under your thumb and the end comes out between your index and middle finger.

11. Bend the wire ends down so they are parallel to each other and perpendicular to the back of the bow. Press the top of your right index finger tight against the underside of the bow between the wires. Holding the wires with the other fingers and palm of your right hand, remove your left thumb and index finger.

12. Grasp the bow loops with your left hand and turn them twice, so that the wires twist tightly between your right index finger and the bow back. Release the loops and give them a fluff.

checking and adjusting your arrangement

When you have completed your design, step back and look it over. Here are some things to check.

- Are the flowers where you want them? Some may have been pushed out of place while you were designing. Each flower deserves its own space. Gently move the main flowers if they are touching one another.
- Is there any paper still on the flowers? Check to be sure that the price tags and the information tags have been removed from the stems.
- If you have cut stems, is the cut concealed?
- If floral foam was used to anchor stems, is the foam completely hidden?
- Do you see any glue or glue strings? Set a hair dryer on hot, and run the air slowly over the design to melt away any glue strings.
- Is the inside of the container clean and free of foam particles? If not, gently lift the arrangement out and clean the container.
- Is the glass free of fingerprints? If not, wet a cloth with white distilled vinegar and wipe the fingerprints away.
- Does the arrangement seem to flow well?
- Are you happy with the result?

cleaning and storing florals

Over time, faux florals can get dusty. You have several options for cleaning them:

Your first option is to use a spray designed specifically for cleaning faux flowers and foliage. Follow the manufacturer's directions for the best results.

If the stems are not in a design, you can also clean them with soap and water. Put warm water and dish soap in a sink or bowl. Have another sink or bowl with water for rinsing. Test one stem first to see how it reacts to the water. Some lose their color; if this happens, use the spray product instead. If not, swish the stem in the soapy water, then in the rinse water. Lay the stems on a cloth and let dry, or blow-dry with a hair dryer on the low, cool setting. A third option is to take your flowers or finished design outside and blow the dust away with a hair dryer.

Before storing a seasonal design, place it in a dark plastic bag so the flowers will retain their color.

You can separate the leftover florals by type, color, or season. Clear plastic, stackable storage boxes allow you to see what's inside, and take up little room. List what's in each container, label the container for easy access, and store them in a dark closet. Today's leftovers are tomorrow's masterpieces, but only if they're in good shape and you know where they are.

designs for *all occasions*

seashore memories

Remember that relaxing day spent gathering shells on the
beach? So many beautiful shells, each so essential to your
collection that soon your pockets were too full to hold any
more. Don't leave your seashore treasures tucked away in a
box where you can't enjoy them. This quick and easy display
will keep those memories fresh. Take it to the office where
it can trigger a soothing daydream when you need a break.

florals

- small bush of sea grass (a)
- green spider mum (b)

tools and materials

- 4½" (11.4 cm) frosted glass cube
- paper-backed, double-sided tape
- 1 cup assorted small shells
- five medium seashells
- 2 cups fine aqua blue sand
- one block ivory rainbow foam
- tube adhesive
- pencil
- scissors
- wire cutter
- knife

1 Wash and dry the vase. Using pencil, draw a line 2" (5 cm) below the top of the vase. Apply the double-sided tape to the vase, aligning the lower edge of the tape to the line. Peel off the paper backing.

2 Press small seashells onto the tape all around the vase, covering as much of the tape as possible. Use tube adhesive to secure extra shells that won't stick to the tape.

3 Cut several tendrils of sea grass from the bush. Press the tendrils here and there along the tape between shells. Use tube adhesive to secure those that won't stick.

4 Cut a 4" × 4" × 3" (10.2 × 10.2 × 7.6 cm) piece of the ivory block foam. Insert the foam into the center of the vase. Fill the space around the foam with fine sand and cover the foam with the sand. This technique uses less sand.

5 Cut the stem of the green spider mum to 3" (7.6 cm). Insert it into the foam to one side of center and push it down until the base touches the sand.

6 Cut the sea grass stem into five parts, one larger than the others. Insert the large part into the foam behind the mum. Insert the other parts into the sand and foam all around the design. Leave some areas open.

7 Add three or four medium-size shells in the open areas and sprinkle with smaller shells to fill in.

8 Look over the design and make any necessary adjustments.

variation: *driftwood*

Fashion a deserted beach in a low, round container with sand, river rocks, and shards of sea glass. Top it with a sandblasted manzanita branch to resemble driftwood, or use actual driftwood if you have it.

wreath topper

Bright flowers and candlelight set the mood for a party. This design shows off a large glass cylinder. Battery-operated candles nestle among blue glass cubes to amplify and reflect their light. For even more drama, the flowers are arranged in a wreath perched on the rim of the cylinder.

florals

- 36" (91.4 cm) ivy garland with vine tendrils **(a)**
- three stems garden roses, each with two flowers and one bud **(b)**
- two stems apricot daisies **(c)**
- three stems small blue flowers **(d)**
- three stems miniature peach branches, each with two peaches and foliage **(e)**

tools and materials

- cylinder vase, 8" tall × 6½" diameter (20.3 × 16.5 cm)
- 10" (25.4 cm) Styrofoam ring
- moss green floral spray paint, if using white Styrofoam
- greening pins
- four colorful scented candles or battery-operated lights
- package of blue glass cubes
- newspaper, gloves, protective mask, and goggles
- glue pan
- scissors
- wire cutter

1 If your Styrofoam is white, you should paint it green. Spread newspaper in a ventilated area. Put on the gloves and protective mask and goggles. Spray the Styrofoam ring with green paint, covering all the surfaces. Allow to dry.

2 Place the Styrofoam ring on top of the glass cylinder and press down gently. Trim the inner ring slightly, if necessary. It should be a snug fit. Remove the wreath from the vase.

3 Cut some of the longer shoots from the ivy vine. Dip the end of the vine into the glue pan and insert it into the side of the ring. Wrap the vine around the ring, securing it with greening pins as you wrap. Insert the cut pieces here and there until the ring is sparsely covered with ivy.

3

7

4

8

4   Cut the roses, leaving stems about 3"
(7.6 cm) long. Insert them evenly spaced
around the ring on the top, outside, and
inside surfaces. Insert them so the flowers
are about ½" (1.3 cm) from the foam.

5   Cut the daisies, leaving the stems about 5"
(12.7 cm) long. Insert them evenly spaced
around the ring on the top, outside, and
inside surfaces. Insert them so the flowers
are about 2" (5 cm) from the foam.

6   Repeat step 5 for the small blue flowers.

7   Cut the peach stems into pieces. Insert the
pieces evenly spaced around the ring among
the flowers.

8   Wash and dry the vase. Gently place the blue
glass cubes into the vase to cover the bottom.
Add battery-operated lights. Then add more
glass cubes around the lights.

9   Turn on the battery operated lights. Replace
the wreath over the rim of the cylinder.

10   Look over the design and make any
necessary adjustments.

split peas

There are lots of clever options for filling glass containers, and they serve more than one purpose. In this design, split peas—straight from the grocery shelf—not only hide the stems, they emphasize the container's unique shape and weight the bottom so it won't tip. Green berry clusters used in the simple garden-style arrangement repeat the color and shape of the peas to unify the design.

florals
- three stems green daisies, each with five flowers (a)
- pink dianthus bush with three stems, each with twelve flowers (b)
- five stems green protea berries (c)

tools and materials
- square glass vase with narrow neck, 4" wide × 9¾" tall (10.2 × 24.8 cm)
- 4 cups dried split green peas
- scissors
- wire cutter

1 Wash and dry the glass vase. Fill the vase to the base of the neck with dried split peas.

2 Open, fluff, and shape the daisy stems. Cut them to about 22" (55.9 cm) long. Insert one stem in the center of the peas and one at each of the four corners, with the stems crisscrossing. This will flare the blossoms out for a rich full view of each daisy.

3 Cut each stem from the dianthus bush, keeping them as long as possible. Insert the stems into the peas at various angles among the daisies.

4 Cut the protea berry stems to about 12" (30.5 cm). Insert one in the center and one in each quadrant of the design.

5 Look over the design and make any necessary adjustments.

from the top

A dozen roses burst from the top of this vase, while their crisscrossed stems fill the base. A hidden foam block at the mouth of the vase keeps everything in place. The foam, concealed by accent flowers and foliage, can easily be removed for dusting and cleaning the vase and simply placed right back on top. Not one stem will fall out of place.

florals

- twelve pink roses **(a)**
- accent flower bush with twelve stems **(b)**
- bush of black olive foliage with twelve stems **(c)**

tools and materials

- rectangular glass vase, 6" × 4" × 9" tall (15.2 × 10.2 × 22.9 cm)
- dry floral foam, large enough to hang over vase top
- four 6" (15.2 cm) wood picks
- glue pan and glue
- tube adhesive
- scissors
- wire cutter
- knife

1 Using a knife, shape the bottom of the foam to fit snugly about ½" (1.3 cm) down into the vase.

2 Remove the wire from the wood picks. Insert the pointed end of the wood pick into the hot glue and then into the foam so the pick is resting on the lip of the vase. Repeat on the other three sides. This will ensure that the foam doesn't slide down into the vase.

3 Leave five rose stems the full length. Hold them up next to the vase and mark the stems even with the top of the foam. Remove all the leaves below this point. Nip off the plastic leaf pegs so the rose stem is smooth.

4

9

4 Working in a ring halfway between the center and the outer edge of the foam, insert five roses so that the stems crisscross below the foam.

5 Cut 2" (5 cm) from the bottom of four rose stems. Remove leaves as in step 3. Working around the first group, insert these roses so the stems crisscross below the foam.

6 Cut the last three stems off 3" (7.6 cm) from the end. Remove leaves as in step 3. Insert these stems into the design where you want more color, texture, and depth.

7 Touch around the insertion point of each stem with a drop of tube adhesive.

8 Cut each of the twelve stems from the accent bush. Insert the stems among and around the rose stems deep into the design. (Some of the stem ends will come through the foam, others may not.)

9 Cut the stems from the black olive bush. Insert the stems tight around the base of the design to hide the foam.

10 Remove the foam from the vase. Wash and dry the glass vase. Replace the foam so the wood picks balance again on the top of the vase.

11 Look over the design and make any necessary adjustments.

votive confidence

This unique metal stand is meant to hold twelve votive candles, but here's a design that is a little more fun. Place the entire stand in a low glass container and cover the base with brightly colored marbles. Instead of candles, fill the votive cups with marbles and gerbera blossoms. Still want candlelight? Add a few tea lights or battery-operated candles among the marbles in the base. Votive holders like these are available at flower shops, and specialty home décor stores.

florals

- ten to twelve gerberas in a variety of colors

tools and materials

- metal votive holder on 6" (15.2 cm) metal base
- twelve glass votive cups
- square glass bowl, 8" wide × 5" tall (20.3 × 12.7 cm)
- 1 cup each of flat marbles in colors to mix and match with gerberas
- glue pan and glue
- scissors
- wire cutter

1 Wash and dry all of the glass containers.

2 Place the metal votive holder into the square glass bowl. Mix all the colors of flat marbles together. Cover the base entirely with marbles.

3

4

3   Place the votive cups into the holders. Fill each votive with marbles to within ¼" (6 mm) of the top.

4   Select gerberas for the votives. Remove the heads. Touch the stems with glue and put the heads back on. Cut the stems to 2" (5 cm). Place a gerbera in each votive so the petals rest on the rims.

5   Look over the design and make any necessary adjustments.

variation: *rose parade*

Cut rose stems so the heads rise slightly above the votive holder rims. Tie each rose just under the head with narrow ribbon streamers. To use fresh roses, be sure to cut the stems under water and fill the base bowl with water mixed with flower food.

serene terrarium

We all love plants, but we don't necessarily love to take care
of them. This terrarium is a decorative conversation piece
that never needs tending. Kids and grown-ups alike will
enjoy peering into the vase to get a closer look at the tranquil
mini–Japanese garden scene. Just for fun, change the scene once
in a while by adding tiny seasonal figures or different plants.

florals

- 2 cups seed pods (a)
- 2 handfuls of green sheet moss (b)
- assorted small pieces of small-leafed greens and berries (c)
- lichens (d)

tools and materials

- square vase, 12" × 12" (30.5 × 30.5 cm), with narrow neck and 5½" (14 cm) rim
- 2 cups river pebbles
- 2 cups light-colored large stones
- 1 cup green glass chips
- four anchor pins
- small bridge
- two miniature men or other figures
- tube adhesive

1 Glue anchor pins to the bottoms of the two miniature figures and to the ends of the bridge, using tube adhesive. Set aside.

2 Wash and dry the vase.

3 Gently place the river pebbles in the bottom of the vase. Next add a layer of seed pods and then a layer of light-colored stones.

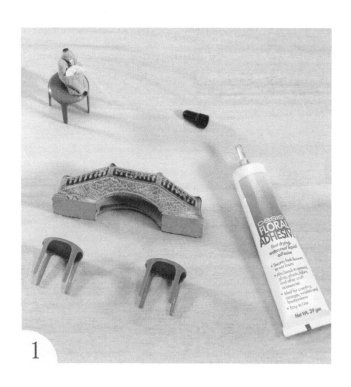

4   Cover the top layer with sheet moss. The layers should come to about the middle of the wide part of the vase.

5   Sprinkle a stream of green glass chips over the moss. Place the bridge over the stream, pushing the anchor pins down into the moss. Add the small figures where you want them.

6   Insert small pieces of foliage to resemble trees, shrubs, and flowers. Add stones, lichens, and any other decorative elements.

7   Look over the design and make any necessary adjustments. Place the terrarium where it can be enjoyed by all!

design tip

Fresh sheet moss is green but if yours has turned brown, lay the moss on newspaper and spray it with a mixture of water and green food coloring. Let it dry before you use it.

tropical trio

Take the classic "three flowers in a bud vase" design, pump it up with warm trade winds and constant sunshine, and you get this lovely tropical trio. This flared square vase is heavy enough to anchor the tall flowers and it has plenty of room for an artistic tangle of wired vines that hold the stems in place.

florals

- three anthurium (**a**)
- two stems Montbretia pod (**b**)
- sago palm (**c**)
- one bush bear grass (**d**)

tools and materials

- glass vase with square bottom and curved sides, 9" (22.9 cm) tall, with 4" (10.2 cm) rim
- floral tape
- 9' (2.7 m) barked wire
- wire cutter

1   Wash and dry the glass vase.

2   In your hand, hold the three anthuriums, one at the top, one in the middle, and one low near your wrist in a zigzag placement. Keep your hand in this position, as this will be even with the top lip of the vase when you cut the stems later. Wrap floral tape twice around the stems to secure.

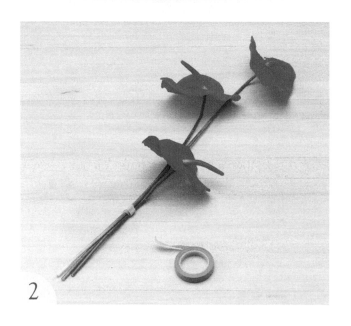

5

6

3 Add the Montbretia pod stems; cut one stem to 6" (15.2 cm), and leave the other long. Refer to the photo for placement. You will cut all of them off at once so they will be close to even. Tape that group onto the first, using floral tape.

4 Add the sago palm and the bear grass; tape them on. Hold the bundle up to the vase so the wrapped tape is even with the lip. Mark a stem even with the vase bottom. Cut off all the stems at this length.

5 Cut 1' (30.5 cm) of barked wire and wrap the stems, covering the taped area.

6 Coil the remaining barked wire by wrapping it around your fingers; place it into the vase and let it uncoil to hug the inside of the vase. Pull some of the end out of the top.

7 Insert the floral bundle, letting the coiled wire support the stems.

8 Look over the design and make any necessary adjustments.

majestic callas

Simplicity can be very impressive. This stately glass vase with a flared rim seems to invite an arrangement with long-stemmed flowers that burst upward with joy. Large callas make a grand statement all on their own. Twists of aluminum wire around their slender stalks hold them together while giving the design an upscale, trendy look.

florals

- twelve large callas

tools and materials

- flared glass vase, 16"
  (40.6 cm) tall
- roll of apple green aluminum wire
- clear anchor tape
- wire cutter

1   Wash and dry the vase.

2   Stand a calla next to the vase and grasp the
    stem with your left hand 3" (7.6 cm) below
    the vase lip. Hold this calla straight up,
    with your thumb facing you. Place a second
    calla across the front at an angle, with the
    head left and tail right. Close your thumb
    over the stem.

3   With your right hand above the left, grasp
    the stems with your right hand, then release
    the left. Now with the flowers in your right
    hand, make a quarter turn toward your body.
    Put the flowers back in your left hand.

4 Repeat steps 2 and 3 with each calla stem, turning the bouquet with each addition. Continue until all the callas are in the bouquet.

5 Still holding the stems securely in your left hand, look at the bouquet and make any adjustments—all the heads should flare outward. Tape the stems together securely with clear anchor tape just above your hand.

6 Cut 2' (61 cm) of wire from the roll. Wrap the wire tightly and close together around the clear tape and down the stems until you come to the end of the wire.

7 Cut another 2' (61 cm) of wire from the roll. Coil the wire and insert it into the base of the vase. Open it up and shape it, drawing loose coils up to the rim.

8 Insert the calla bundle so the wire trails around the stems and helps support them.

9 Look over the design and make any necessary adjustments.

design tip

This design tends to be a little top heavy. For extra stability, place clear glass marbles in the bottom or add distilled water up to the level of the wrapped wire. This design works great with fresh callas, too. Simply fill the vase with fresh water and flower food. The aluminum wire doesn't affect the water quality.

peacock pride

Cobalt glass pieces are stunning accents to your décor, and you'll find many cobalt containers that are suitable for floral designs. In this elegant arrangement, the deep blue glass plays up the eyes of these peacock feathers. This fan-shaped vase has a narrow opening, so the bells of Ireland stalks and peacock feathers need no other support.

florals
- nine stems bells of Ireland
- fifteen to twenty peacock feathers

tools and materials
- cobalt blue flared vase, 10" tall × 9" wide (25.4 × 22.9 cm) with 2" (5 cm) rim (measured from front to back)
- scissors
- wire cutter

1 Wash and dry the vase.

2 Cut the stems of the bells of Ireland so that when they are inserted into the vase, the lowest blossom will touch the vase lip.

3 Insert the bells of Ireland into the vase so they form a fan. The stems will interlock in the vase.

4 Cut the ends of seven feathers so the eye of the feather is just above the flower stems. Insert the feathers in a fan shape, fairly evenly spaced.

5 Cut the ends of three or four feathers so the eye of the feather rests just above the lip of the vase. Insert these feathers low in front, following the fan shape.

6 Cut the remaining feathers so their eyes will be halfway between the other two rows of feathers. Insert these feathers.

7 Look over the design and make any necessary adjustments.

glads all over

Monochromatic designs don't have to be boring. Textural
contrasts become much more apparent when all the elements
are the same color. Here spiky French gladiolus stalks with soft,
fluted blossoms generate plenty of energy. Your eyes rest on the
fuzzy, prickly echinacea seed pods before traveling down into the
tangle of thin branches that support the stems. No ho-hum here!

florals

- one stem of wired branches **(a)**
- twelve stems French gladiolus **(b)**
- two stems echinacea, each with four flower heads **(c)**

tools and materials

- glass cylinder, 12" tall × 5" diameter (30.5 × 12.7 cm)
- scissors
- wire cutter

2

3

1 Wash and dry the vase.

2 Cut the wired branches from the main stem.
   Holding two or three at a time, twist and
   shape the branches to resemble a root
   system and place them in the bottom of
   the vase.

3 Cut 2" (5 cm) from the bottom of each
   gladiolus stem. Insert them into the vase
   with the stems all parallel, straight up and
   down around the inside of the vase.

4 Cut the stems of the echinacea so the flower
   heads will rest close to the vase rim. Insert them
   around the vase rim, with stems parallel to the
   gladioli, for a contrast in texture and to help
   support the gladioli.

5 Look over the design and make any
   necessary adjustments.

fresh idea

Coil live curly willow branches in your hand
and put them into the vase first to support
fresh gladiolus stems. Fill the vase with fresh
water and flower food. Add fresh echinacea
blossoms around the rim.

daisies in grass

You can have springtime indoors, even in the middle of winter.
This delightful little section of lawn will cheer up any room—and
it doesn't need to be mowed! Make several of them for greater
effect. Scattered daisies, rising above the green blades, turn their
faces toward the sun while the clear glass sides of the container
invite you to peek at what's going on at ground level.

florals

- sheet moss
- grass mat
- two stems white mini daisies, each with multiple blossoms

tools and materials

- square glass bowl, 8" × 3½" tall (20.3 × 8.95 cm)
- ½ cup river pebbles
- scissors
- wire cutter

1 Wash and dry the glass bowl.

2 Lay a thin layer of sheet moss in the bowl, right side up.

3 Cut the grass mat to fit the bowl. Insert it over the moss.

3

4 Place more moss around the sides of the bowl with the right side facing out.

5 Drop a few pebbles around the sides of the vase so they are visible from the sides.

6 Cut the daisy stems apart into separate stems. Trim one-third of the stems to 3" (7.6 cm), one-third of the stems to 4" (10.2 cm) and the rest to 5" (12.7 cm). Insert the daisies randomly in the grass.

7 Look over the design and make any necessary adjustments.

design idea

Create a springtime mood any time with jonquils, daffodils, daisies, or tulips.

orchids and apples

These unusual stemmed goblet vases could be used to hold
floating candles or flower blossoms. In this design, aluminum
wire complements the green color of the apples and orchids
and defines the graceful arc of the orchid stems.

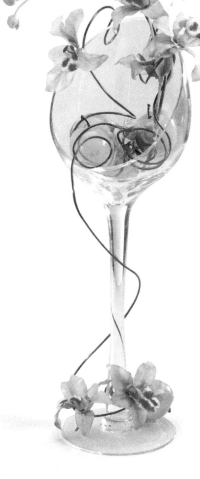

florals

- twelve small green apples
- three stems cymbidium orchids

tools and materials

- two goblet vases, 15" and 10" tall (38.1 and 25.4 cm)
- aluminum wire
- jewelry needle-nose pliers
- glue dots

1 Wash and dry the goblets.

2 Place six green apples in the shorter goblet, securing them to the glass and to each other with glue dots.

3 Repeat step 2 with the taller goblet and five apples. Secure one apple to the foot of the goblet.

4 Cut aluminum wire into five 24" (61 cm) pieces. Using the pliers, bend double spirals in the ends of all the wires.

5 Cut a length of orchid stem that has five blossoms, including the buds at the tip. Loosely entwine the stem with one of the

5

6

wires, guiding the buds through the spiral at one end of the wire. Form the rest of the wire into a tangle of loops. Secure the wired stem to the top of the short goblet, using a glue dot on the back rim. Arch the stem so it comes over the left side in front of the apples. Bend the end spiral down along the back of the goblet.

6 Using another wire, weave one end among the apples in the short goblet; bring it out of the front and coil it loosely down to the foot of the goblet. Secure an orchid blossom to the end spiral at the goblet foot, using a glue dot. Tuck another blossom among the apples.

7 Entwine two longer orchid stems with two wires, again guiding the bud ends through the spirals of the wire ends. Tangle the ends of the wires together loosely and weave them among the apples in the tall goblet. Arch the stems from the right side up out of the goblet; one down and to the left, the other back to the left. Secure with glue dots.

8

8 Coil the last wire from the goblet bowl loosely around the stem to the foot. Glue two blossoms near the apple at the base.

9 Look over the design and make any necessary adjustments.

tulip swish

Nothing says spring like tulips. This lovely bunch,
bending gracefully over a tall oval glass container,
seems to have sprouted through melting snow. This
is a very easy design to put together, and it would
make a cheerful, long-lasting gift for a friend.

florals

- six tulips
- two green spring branch stems

tools and materials

- oval glass vase, 10" wide × 7" tall (25.4 × 17.8 cm) with 2½" (6.4 cm) rim
- 2 cups clear beads
- 24" (61 cm) pink double-faced satin ribbon, 1½" (3.8 cm) wide
- glue dots
- scissors
- wire cutter

1 Wash and dry the vase. Carefully pour the clear beads into the vase.

2 Cut the tulip stems so the total lengths, including blossoms, are as follows: one 12" (30.5 cm), two 11" (27.9 cm), two 10" (25.4 cm), and one 9" (22.9 cm).

3 Insert the longest tulip about 2" (5 cm) from the left corner and allow the stem to arch toward the right and droop down over the vase rim.

4 Continue to insert tulips, longest to shortest, stacking them loosely and all arching in the same direction. Turn some heads slightly back or forward.

4

5

6

5 Cut the branch into separate stems. Place them in and around the tulip stems for a natural look.

6 Place a glue dot on the bottom of the vase one-third of the distance from the left side.

7 Lay the ribbon on the design surface and place the vase over the center of the ribbon, aligning it with the glue dot. Bring the ribbon straight up the sides. Tie the ends in a square knot. Then tie the ends in a bow, if desired, or trim them and let them hang over the sides of the vase.

8 Look over the design and make any necessary adjustments.

7

tulip high-rise

A tall, pilsner-style vase is the basis for this grand floral design.
Large parrot tulips climb through a cloud of hydrangeas and
reach for the sky. Because the flower stems and branches would
not be long enough to reach down into the bottom of the vase,
you need a creative way to arrange them. Floral foam wrapped
in large leaves is wedged into the vase to provide hidden
support for branches and flowers above and below the rim.

florals

- seven artificial birch branches
  (substitute fresh or dry, if desired)
  (a)
- two aspidistra leaves **(b)**
- nine long-stem parrot tulips **(c)**
- five dark blue hydrangeas **(d)**
- four white hydrangeas **(e)**

tools and materials

- pilsner-glass vase,
  26" (66 cm) tall
- one block dry floral foam
- anchor tape
- glue pan
- utility snips
- scissors
- wire cutter
- knife

1   Arrange all the floral materials on your design surface in groups according to type.

2   Cut a piece of foam large enough to wedge into the neck of the vase, so the top will extend above the vase at least 1" (2.5 cm). Remove the plastic veins from the aspidistra leaves. Wrap the leaves, right side out, around the foam, and secure with glue. Wedge the foam into the vase.

3   Cut 2" (5 cm) from the bottom of three tulip stems; leave the remaining tulips long. Insert one of the long tulips into the center of the foam, straight up. Insert the rest of the long tulips, one at a time, so they all radiate from the center of the foam but angle outward in all directions, fairly evenly spaced.

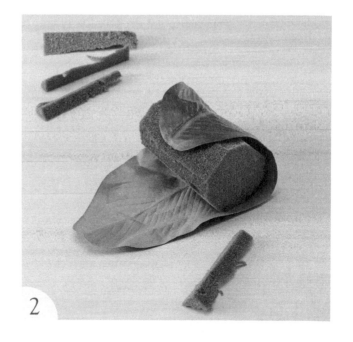

3

5

4 Insert the short tulips outside the other stems, so they arch out to the sides of the design, one in each third of the circumference.

5 Open and shape four of the birch branches for a natural look. Insert the stems among the tulips stems so they appear to radiate from the center.

6 Carefully remove the design from the vase and set it aside while you wash and dry the vase.

7 Insert the remaining birch branches, tip down, into the vase and mark where they meet the vase lip. Remove the branches and cut them off at the mark.

9

8 Insert the branches, cut end up, into the foam from the bottom of the design. Then insert the branches and the foam into the vase.

9 Cut the stems of the hydrangea to 6" (15.2 cm). Remove all the foliage. Insert the flower heads around the base of the design, extending out over the vase rim.

10 Look over the design and make any necessary adjustments.

cobalt duet

Hydrangeas and cobalt blue glass are best friends. Fill a small
pitcher with clear marbles. Add some lily of the valley stems for
texture contrast and you've got a winning combination. Double
the impact with a look-alike arrangement in a similar pitcher
filled with ice chips. They'd be great for a Mother's Day tea or
a spring bridal shower!

florals

- two hydrangea stems **(a)**
- eight hydrangea leaves **(b)**
- ten stems lily of the valley **(c)**

tools and materials

- two similar glass pitchers with cobalt blue handles, 7" (17.8 cm) tall
- 2 cups clear marbles
- 2 cups small artificial ice chips
- sheer ribbon, 1½" (3.8 cm) wide
- floral tape
- glue pan
- scissors

1 Wash and dry the pitchers. Fill one pitcher to just below the neck with clear glass marbles. Put ice chips in the other pitcher to the same level.

2 Cut the hydrangea stems so, when inserted into the pitcher, the flower heads will rest on the rim.

3 Glue leaves around the base of each hydrangea head, right side up, forming a collar.

4

6

4   Insert the lily of the valley stems down into a hydrangea head. Wrap floral tape around the stems to secure into a bundle. Arrange the other bundle with the lily of the valley stems around the hydrangea head.

5   Cut four 9" (22.9 cm) lengths of ribbon. Wrap one length around the stems of each bundle to hide the floral tape; secure with a touch of glue.

6   Insert a bundle into each pitcher. Tie a knot in the center of each of the two remaining ribbon lengths and tie small knots in the ends. Glue the center knots down inside the hydrangea heads and let the streamers flow out.

7   Look over the design and make any necessary adjustments.

fresh idea

Make fresh bundles by inserting lily of the valley from your garden down into fresh hydrangea heads. Make a collar of fresh hydrangea leaves and wrap with clear anchor tape. Put them in pitchers of fresh water with flower food.

thrills and spills

The interesting shape of this vase is emphasized by the frosted surfaces around the bottom. Stems or vines down inside the vase would draw attention away from its beautiful shape, so all of the florals for this design are arranged at the top. Being able to see through the vase and catch a glimpse of the flowers and leaves trailing down on the other side makes it even more intriguing.

florals

- three stems purple lisianthus, each with three blossoms (a)
- three stems peach lisianthus, each with three blossoms (b)
- purple berry bush with fourteen berry clusters (c)
- purple spiderwort bush (d)

tools and materials

- glass vase, 9" (22.9 cm) tall, with heavy diamond-shaped bottom and curved sides
- one-third block of dry floral foam
- 2 yd. (1.85 m) purple wired ribbon, 1½" (3.8 cm) wide
- six 3" (7.6 cm) wood picks
- scissors
- wire cutter
- knife

1 Cut and shape the foam so it fits snugly into the rim of the vase, one-third below the rim and two-thirds above. Wedge the foam into the vase. If additional support is needed, remove the wires from four wood picks, and insert the picks into the foam from the side so they rest on the vase rim.

2 Cut the two lowest lisianthus blossoms from each stem, leaving the stems as long as possible. Beginning with the purple lisianthus, insert the longest stems to the right side, draping to within 6" (15.2 cm) of the design surface. Continue inserting stems, longest to shortest, alternating the directions of their heads, but all extending to the right side of the vase. The shortest stems will be near the center top of the design.

4

6

3 Repeat step 2 with the peach lisianthus, inserting them to drape off the left side of the vase.

4 Cut the berry bush into separate stems. Insert the berries throughout the design, longest stems draping outward to right and left, shorter stems nearer the center.

5 Cut the spiderwort bush into separate stems, leaving them as long as possible. Insert the longest stems into the base of the foam so they drape down below the lisianthus to the right and left. Insert the remaining stems between flowers and berries wherever they are needed to conceal the foam.

6 Cut the ribbon in half. Make a loop in the center of one half and secure the base of the loop with the wire of a wood pick. Wrap the wire tail tightly around the wood pick. Repeat for the other ribbon. Insert one wood pick into the front right side; insert the other into the back left side. Style the tails and loop.

7 Remove the foam from the vase. Wash and dry the vase. Replace the foam so the wood picks balance again on the top of the vase.

8 Look over the design and make any necessary adjustments.

wired orchids

If you want to draw attention to something, put it behind glass and under water. Here orchids strung on aluminum wire look amazingly lifelike. Submersible lights heighten the impact, especially in the evening. Most permanent botanicals don't mind getting wet, but it is a good idea to submerge one of the flowers in water to test for any negative effects.

florals

- seven stems medium cymbidium orchids
- two cymbidium buds

tools and materials

- glass cylinder, 18" tall × 6" diameter (45.7 × 15.2 cm)
- 2 cups synthetic copper stones
- five submersible lights
- 3 yd. (2.75 m) aluminum wire
- glue gun and glue or tube adhesive
- awl
- scissors
- wire cutter

1   Wash and dry the vase.

2   Gently place the copper stones into the bottom of the cylinder. Set the submersible lights, evenly spaced, on the stones.

3   Cut the orchid blossoms off of their stems. Using an awl, pierce a hole in the back of each blossom and bud. Thread the blossoms onto the wire, going through the holes.

2

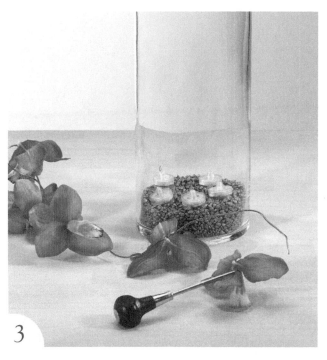

3

4

4 Position all of the blossoms and buds along the wire. Secure each in place with a drop of hot glue. You can also use tube adhesive, but it takes a little longer to dry.

5 Coil and twist the wire and place it inside the cylinder.

6 When it is time to light the design, turn on the submersible lights and push them down into the stones, covering the bases. The lights will last for three days under water.

7 Slowly fill the cylinder with water. The blossoms and buds will look like fresh flowers.

8 Look over the design and make any necessary adjustments.

9 Change the water often to avoid a ring of mineral deposits. Insert new batteries into the lights as needed. When you want to disassemble the design, pat the flowers with a towel and lay them out to air dry.

variation: *orchid contempo*

Entwine six stems of dendrobium orchids, end to end, with black aluminum wire, forming a garland. Arrange the garland inside a contemporary oval vase in a crescent shape. Drape the last stems and wire in a graceful arc out of the vase and curving down to the table.

tulips through twigs

Like natural tulips forcing their way up through the soil,
this design has a quiet grace. Three flashes of red grab your
attention while pebbles, roots, and bulbs deep inside the
vase invite a closer look. Notice how the gentle curves of the
vase echo the shapes of the bulbs and their emerging leaf stalks.

florals

- green sheet moss
- three artificial tulip bulbs with hole in center
- three tulips
- birch branches or other natural-looking twigs

tools and materials

- glass hurricane vase, 12" (30.5 cm) tall
- small stones
- glue pan
- scissors
- wire cutter
- utility snips

1 Wash and dry the hurricane vase. Gently place stones in the bottom of the vase. Lay a shallow layer of moss over the stones.

2 Cut the tulips to 12", 9", and 6" (30.5, 22.9, and 15.2 cm). Glue the stem end of each tulip into a bulb.

2

4

3 Set the tulips and bulbs into the vase, equally spaced.

4 Cut birch branches to various lengths, all taller than the vase. Insert the branches into the vase around the inside so they visually protect the tulips. Push the stems down through the moss into the stones for support.

5 Look over the design and make any necessary adjustments.

variation: *twig fence*

Stand twigs around the outside of a short glass cylinder, holding them in place with a rubber band. Cut individual flower stems from a seasonal mixed bush, and add them among the twigs. Secure the stems by wrapping the cylinder with barked wire; then snip off the rubber band. Float a candle for ambience.

dynamic curves

Create some excitement with a swayback square vase, curly stems, and spectacular giant roses. The ingredient list for this recipe is short, but the stunning results will hold your attention for a long time. Dried, curly stems, called Panchu springs, keep your eyes moving from down inside the vase up into the flowers. Never a dull moment!

florals
- one bunch (ten stems) colored Panchu springs **(a)**
- seven roses **(b)**
- berry and grass bush with six stems **(c)**

tools and materials
- square glass vase with curved sides, 9" tall × 4" wide (22.9 × 10.2 cm)
- scissors
- wire cutter

1 Wash and dry the vase.

2 Insert the curly ends of some of the Panchu springs down into the vase. Let them follow their own arrangement. Bring some curls out the top and down the sides of the vase.

3 Cut the roses to various lengths, the longest at 22" (55.9 cm), two at 18" (45.7 cm), two at 16" (40.6 cm) and two at 12" (30.5 cm). Insert them into the vase, arranging the stems in and through the Panchu spring curls; the tallest just off center, the shortest to the lower front corner.

4 Separate the berry and grass bush into individual stems. Cut off any plastic pegs that held stems or foliage. Add the stems randomly throughout the design.

5 Look over the design and make any necessary adjustments.

exotic tower

Exotic tropical flowers have a place in almost any décor at any time of year. In this simple design, the tall agapanthus flowers are balanced by the orchids and leaves near the rim of the vase. The fluted glass vase has both the physical and visual weight to anchor this design. Strong textural contrasts keep your eyes traveling in a triangle.

florals

- three monstera leaves (a)
- three stems tall agapanthus (b)
- two stems phaleonopsis orchids (c)
- two stems sago palm (d)

tools and materials

- clover leaf vase, 8" tall × 4" wide
  (20.3 × 10.2 cm)
- sea glass, light and dark green
- dry floral foam
- white distilled vinegar
- anchor pin
- aisle runner tape
- double-sided tape
- scissors
- wire cutter
- knife

1 Wash and dry the vase. Swab the inside bottom with distilled vinegar to remove any traces of oil.

2 Cut a 2" (5 cm) piece of aisle runner tape and secure it to the inside bottom of the vase. Place a small piece of double-sided tape on the bottom of the anchor pin, and secure the anchor pin to the center of the vase bottom.

3 Cut foam to fit inside the vase to 2" (5 cm) below the rim. Secure it to the bottom of the vase over the anchor pin.

4 Remove the plastic vein from one monstera leaf. Wrap the leaf, right side out, around the foam.

5   Leave the stems of the agapanthus as long as possible and insert them parallel to each other in the back left side of the vase.

6   Cut the stem of one monstera leaf so the entire leaf base is resting on the vase to the left side. Cut the second stem to 9" (22.9 cm). Bend the leaf flat from the stem and insert it just above the previous leaf, shadowing it.

7   Cut one orchid stem 4" (10.2 cm) below the lowest blossom; cut the other stem 5" (12.7 cm) below the lowest blossom. Insert the longest stem first coming out of the right front, flowing gently up and over the lip of the vase. Insert the second one above it, shadowing the placement of the first.

8   Cut the stem of one sago palm to 3" (7.6 cm) and insert it behind the agapanthus stems. Cut the stem of the other sago slightly longer. Bend and curl the foliage, forming an arch, and insert it in the same spot as the first one, shadowing its placement.

9   Fill the vase with sea glass for color and to help weight the base of the design.

10   Look over the design and make any necessary adjustments.

marching stems

A uniquely shaped vase calls for an unusual floral design. Six stunning gerberas march in sync along the length of the oval opening. Though all of the elements are orange, there is nothing boring about the combination because of the contrast of textures.

florals

- six sawtooth gerberas
- one euphorbia stem, 47" (14.3 cm) long

tools and materials

- oval glass vase, 9" tall × 2" wide (22.9 × 5 cm)
- 2 cups flat marbles in color to match gerberas
- glue dots
- scissors
- wire cutter

1 Wash and dry the vase.

2 Measure one gerbera so, when inserted straight up and down into the vase, the petals will rest on the rim. Cut the stem. Cut the stems of the other gerberas to the same length.

3 Gently place the marbles into the vase. Even them out so the surface is flat.

4 Wrap the euphorbia stem around the rim of the vase, beginning on the inside and finishing on the outside. Secure here and there with glue dots.

5 Place the gerberas into the vase in a row, evenly spaced and all straight up and down. The petals will overlap slightly.

6 Look over the design and make any necessary adjustments.

designs for *special events*

look but don't touch

Show off brightly colored glass Christmas ornaments inside a large glass vase. The sparkle is so eye-catching and the colors are so festive! Roses, hydrangeas, and glass grapes peek out unexpectedly here and there. Yet, the glass keeps inquisitive fingers away. This design provides a panoramic view, so you could display it on a low coffee table or in front of a mirror in a foyer.

florals

- twelve rosebuds **(a)**
- five glass grape clusters **(b)**
- two stems green hydrangea **(c)**

tools and materials

- barrel-shaped glass vase, 15" tall × 6" to 8" wide (38.1 × 15.2 to 20.3 cm)
- forty-eight glass ornaments, 1" to 1¼" (25 to 30 mm)
- twenty-five glass ornaments, 1½" (40 mm)
- glue dots
- 4 yd. (3.7 m) each of sheer unwired ribbon in pink, red, and lime green, 1½" (3.8 cm) wide
- floral tape
- one 24-gauge floral wire, 18" (45.7 cm) long
- wire cutter

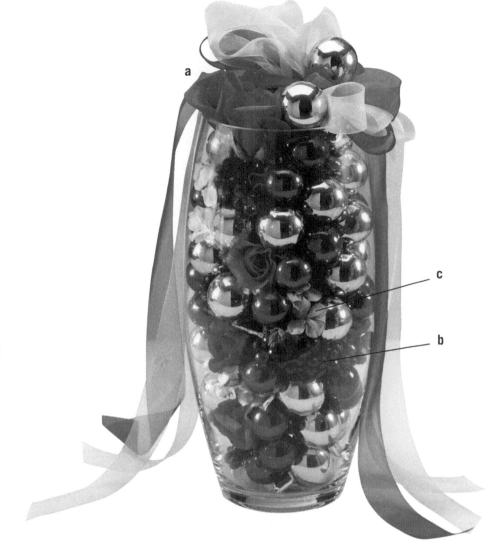

1 Wash and dry the vase. Remove all the hooks and wires that may be on the ornaments.

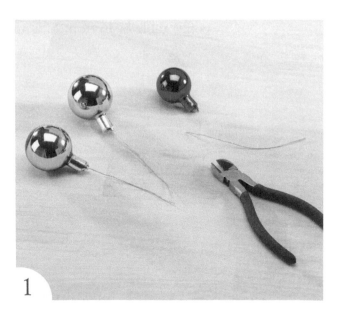

2

2 Start placing ornaments carefully into the vase, one at a time, so the hanger ends always face inward. As you fill to the top, add a rose, hydrangea, or grape cluster here and there. Remember, the design will be seen from all sides, so turn ornaments and florals toward the outside where they will be most visible. Use glue dots to secure any ornaments that rise above the rim.

3 Fold the floral wire in half and wrap it with floral tape. Make a large floppy bow with long streamers, using all three ribbons, and tie the bow with the wire.

3

4 Insert the wire carefully down into the vase and allow the tails to stream out over the edge of the vase.

5 Look over the design and make any necessary adjustments.

design tip

Do you have antique ornaments that are too precious to hang on the tree where little hands can reach them? Displaying them in a large glass vase keeps them out of reach but in full view.

holiday housewarmer

Low square glass bowls are very common. You can use them for serving dishes or to float candles or fresh flowers. Here's a way to turn one of these ordinary containers into an attractive holiday hostess gift, using simple ornaments and floral candle rings.

florals

- two poinsettia candle rings,
  3" (7.6 cm) diameter

tools and materials

- low square glass bowl with
  slanted or straight sides, 8"
  (20.3 cm) rim
- about 20 red ball ornaments,
  2" (5 cm) diameter
- one block dry floral foam
- anchor pin
- aisle runner tape
- paper-backed double-sided tape
- glue pan
- glue dots
- scissors
- knife

1 Wash and dry the glass bowl. Cut a 2"
(5 cm) square of aisle runner tape and
secure it to the bottom center of the bowl.

2 Cut a 1" (2.5 cm) piece of double-sided tape
and secure it to the underside of the anchor
pin. Remove the paper backing and secure
the pin to the center of the runner tape.

3 Cut a 2" × 2" × 4" (5.1 × 5.1 × 10.2 cm)
piece of dry floral foam. Dip one end in
hot glue and secure it upright to the
anchor pin.

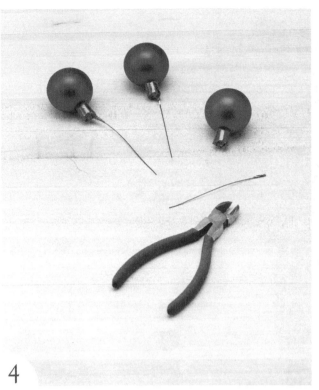

4

5

4 Remove wired caps from the tops of the ball ornaments or cut off wire stems.

5 Arrange ornaments in two layers in the bottom of the bowl, turning the tops toward the foam.

6 Place a candle ring over the ornaments circling the foam.

7 Cut the remaining candle ring into pieces, leaving stems as long as possible. Insert the stems into open spaces, alternating with ornaments. Secure stems into the foam with a touch of hot glue or secure pieces to each other using glue dots.

8 Look over the design and make any necessary adjustments.

6

amaryllis and cherries

Celebrate the holidays with an elegant amaryllis design. Ornaments
and cherries fill the clear glass vase, providing visual weight for the
base. The vase itself has a heavy bottom, necessary to prevent tipping
of this tall arrangement. Cherry garland curves gracefully around
the tall stems, drawing your eyes to the vibrant red blossoms of
the amaryllis.

florals

- cherry garland,
  6' (1.8 m) long **(a)**
- two stems amaryllis **(b)**

tools and materials

- square vase with heavy base and
  shaped sides, 10" (25.4 cm) tall
  with 4½" (11.4 cm) rim
- six 2" (5 cm) ornaments
- three 1¼" (3 cm) ornaments
- glue gun and glue
- scissors
- wire cutter

1 Wash and dry the vase.

2 Cut the cherry garland in half and cut
   the small cherry stems from one half of
   the garland.

3 Set the amaryllis stems in the vase, and
   hold them upright in the center of the
   opening. Tie or tape the stems together just
   below the blossoms.

4   Place the loose cherries and 2" (5 cm) ornaments randomly in the vase, supporting the amaryllis stems.

5   Wrap the remaining cherry garland around the amaryllis stems and down into the vase.

6   Glue the small ornaments and cherries into the amaryllis blossoms for additional texture and light.

7   Look over the design and make any necessary adjustments.

fresh idea

Create the same arrangement with fresh amaryllis stems. Use fresh cherries or cranberries along with ornaments to fill the vase and support the stems. Fill with fresh water with flower food.

ice-cream soda

Perfect for a summer party or special event, these
ice-cream soda floral arrangements look good enough to
eat! The rainbow floral foam comes in bright colors that
look like sherbet or ice cream mounded in a soda glass.
Frilly carnations are the whipped cream and an artificial
strawberry in a pretend puddle of chocolate completes
the illusion. For an entertaining party activity, have
your guests design their own sodas. They're fat free!

florals

- small to medium faux strawberry, blackberry, or cherry
- three to five standard carnations in color of choice

tools and materials

- soda glass
- ice-cream scoop
- two crazy straws
- plastic spoon
- October brown floral spray paint
- sheet of plastic
- rubber gloves, protective mask, and goggles
- powdered rainbow foam in three colors
- brick rainbow foam in desired color
- tube adhesive
- glue pan and glue
- scissors
- wire cutter

1 Heat the glue in the glue pan to 125°F (50°C). Dip the berry into the warm glue as you would dip a berry in chocolate. Place the berry in its glue puddle on a sheet of plastic, and allow the glue to cool.

2 Peel the cooled berry from the plastic. Put on a rubber glove and hold the berry in your fingertips with the glue-covered area exposed. Spray the glue puddle and the glue-covered area of the berry with brown paint. Set the berry aside to dry.

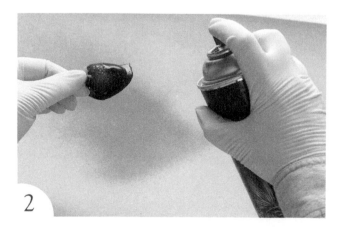

3

5

3 Wash and dry the soda glass. Put half a handful of the first color of rainbow foam into the bottom of the glass. Repeat with the other two colors. Press down on each layer to compact the rainbow foam slightly.

4 Cut the carnation stems to 6" (15.2 cm) long, including the blossom. Save one of the stem pieces for step 5. Insert each carnation into the soda glass at a slight angle inward to keep the stems from showing. Place them low so the flowers hang down a little over the lip of the glass.

5 Using the ice-cream scoop, dip out a scoop of the brick rainbow foam. Insert one of the cut carnation stem ends into the scoop; insert the opposite end into the layered powdered foam.

6 Add two funky straws, and a spoon. Top off the design with the chocolate-covered berry, glued in place with a drop of tube adhesive.

7 Look over the design and make any necessary adjustments.

fresh idea

This design can be made with fresh carnations. When you layer foam in the glass, don't compress it. Add water mixed with flower food. Then cut fresh carnations and insert them into the wet foam. Accent the design with foam scoops and utensils in the same way.

totally tubular

Tube-shaped glass containers, whether intended as vases or not, can be used with faux florals in lots of ingenious ways. Some come with their own stand for tabletop display. Use them to make place-setting designs for a shower or birthday party. Fill tubes with colored marbles or beads to hide not-so-perfect stems. Or leave them just as they are for a more contemporary look.

Reclining holders. Choose single, impressive flower blossoms for smaller containers. Fill the tubes with shiny glass marbles or beads in colors to accent the flowers. These would make great individual place-setting designs.

Upright holders. Change the holder with a coat of spray paint, if you like. Here three roses are arranged in traditional fashion in one tube. Tall, bare-stemmed gerberas are a bit more unconventional.

Welcome spring mobile. This mobile was intended to hold snapshots. Instead of photos, hang a floral water tube from each clip and add your favorite spring flowers.

lighted lily

For a striking but quick and easy place-setting design, "float" a lighted water lily in a large, stemmed glass container. For instance, you could use a large margarita glass. The water is really glass marbles, which makes it easy to use this design in multiples. Lily lights, available where other floral products are sold, are permanent botanical water lilies with submersible LED lights secured to the center. If you are unable to find them, you can simply secure a submersible light to the center of any large blossom with a flat base. Add sheer ribbon for the ultimate finishing touch.

florals

- lily light or water lily and submersible light

tools and materials

- pedestal container, 8" (20.3 cm) tall with 5½" (14 cm)-diameter bowl
- 1 cup glass marbles
- 1 yd. (0.92 m) sheer light green ribbon, 1½" (3.8 cm) wide
- 1 yd. (0.92 m) sheer silver ribbon, 1½" (3.8 cm) wide
- glue dots

1 Wash and dry the container.

2 Gently place the marbles into the container. Place the lily light on top of the marbles.

3 Hold both ribbons together behind the glass stem, with about two-thirds of the length to one side. Bring the ribbons to the front and twist them once. Then bring the ribbons to the sides and over the top. Secure with glue dots, if you prefer. Tie in a bow, off-center, over the lily, letting the ends fall to the sides.

4 When it is time to light the lily, gently slide the ribbons over to remove the lily, turn on the light, and replace the lily. Then slide the ribbons back in place. Separate the green and silver layers.

5 Look over the design and make any necessary adjustments.

blossom bridge

Clear or frosted glass cubes are used for this design. Connect just
two or connect a few. Run them down the center of your table for
a dinner party. They show off the rainbow foam, which fits snugly
into them. For a wedding design, like this one, I chose the ivory
foam, but it comes in so many colors you can have a little fun with
your choices. Once connected, the cubes are a little difficult to
move, so plan and prepare your floral materials first and then put
your design together at the table.

florals

- two stems white dendrobium orchids (a)
- one stem palm seed vine, 35" (88.9 cm) long (b)
- four white roses (c)
- two stems variegated dieffenbachia (d)

tools and materials

- two square glass vases, 4½" wide × 3½" tall (11.4 × 8.9 cm)
- clear double-sided tape
- pearl garland trim
- one block ivory rainbow foam
- scissors
- wire cutter
- knife

1 Wash and dry the vases. Apply double-sided tape around the upper edge of each vase. Secure pearl garland to the tape.

2 Using a large knife, cut the ivory foam block into two pieces that will fit the vases tightly. Insert them into the vases and cut them off even with the tops of the vases.

3 Cut the orchid stems to 3" (7.6 cm) below the last blossom. Insert a stem into the center of each foam cube so the lowest blossom is resting on the foam.

4

5

6

4   Set the vases about 1' (30.5 cm) apart on the design surface. Bend the orchid stems toward each other and entwine the stems and blossoms to form an arch.

5   Cut the four longest stems from the palm seed vine. Insert two stems into each vase, one on each side of the orchid stem. Entwine the palm seed vines around the orchid stems.

6   Cut the stems of the roses about 2" (5 cm) long. Insert them around the point of radiation in both vases. Repeat with the dieffenbachia leaves.

7   Look over the design and make any necessary adjustments.

fresh idea

Rainbow foam can also be used for fresh flowers. Prepare the vases in the same way. Mix flower food in fresh water and pour into the vases until the foam is fully saturated. Then create the design with fresh orchid stems.

autumn cascade

The glorious colors of autumn leaves and flowers are also fleeting. Permanent botanicals, however, never lose their brilliance. This lavish display of fall florals will help you celebrate this all-too-short season from late August through Thanksgiving. The design is anchored in floral foam attached to a Lomey saucer and pedestal, which fits down inside the Eiffel Tower vase. The splayed foot of this tall, slim vase makes it surprisingly stable.

florals

- ivy garland, 6' (1.8 m) long **(a)**
- six sunflowers **(b)**
- two bunches autumn spike bush, each with nine stems **(c)**
- two stems small orange lily **(d)**
- nine yellow rosebuds **(e)**
- two berry bunches, each with six stems **(f)**
- bunch purple foxtail with nine stems **(g)**

tools and materials

- clear Eiffel Tower vase
- 21" (53.3 cm) Lomey pedestal
- 6" (15.2 cm) clear Lomey saucer
- Lomey adhesive
- one-third block floral foam
- two anchor pins
- aisle runner tape
- clear anchor tape, ¼" (6 mm) wide
- tube adhesive

1. Wash and dry the vase, pedestal, and saucer. Glue the 6" (15.2 cm) saucer onto the pedestal using the Lomey adhesive. Allow to dry, following the manufacturer's directions.

2. Cut 4" (10.2 cm) of aisle runner tape and adhere it to the center of the saucer. Apply tube adhesive to the rough sides of the anchor pins and adhere them 1" (2.5 cm) from each end of the aisle runner tape. Allow to dry.

3. Gently push the one-third block of foam onto the anchor pins. Wrap clear anchor tape around the foam and saucer several times in all directions. Insert the pedestal into the vase.

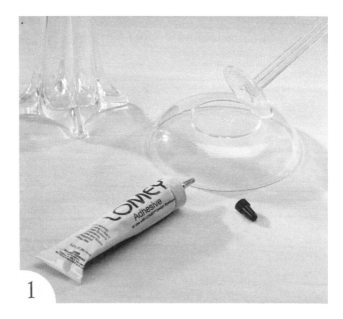

1

4

5

7

4 Cut the ivy into individual stems and insert them all around the base. Cut the sunflower stems to 6" (15.2 cm) and insert them evenly spaced all around the design.

5 Cut the autumn spike bush into separate stems. Insert each stem into the foam, draping down over the sides of the saucer all around the base of the design.

6 Cut the small orange lilies into individual stems, and insert them evenly spaced into the design.

7 Cut four roses to 12" (30.5 cm), four to 10" (25.4 cm), and one to 8" (20.3 cm). Insert the rose stems in and around the design. Use the photo as a placement guide.

8 Cut apart the berry bunches and foxtail bunches into individual stems 6" to 9" (15.2 to 22.9 cm) long. Insert the stems in and around the design, filling in all the space.

9 Turn the design, viewing it from all directions. Make any necessary adjustments.

candy corn

Have a little fun with glass containers that nest inside of each other.
You'll find both square and circular containers that come in graduated
sizes, perfect for making quick and easy displays like this Halloween
treat. Make them as party favors for your guests, or make one in a
larger size for a centerpiece.

florals

- chrysanthemum (a)
- yarrow (b)
- dahlia (c)
- three stems small cattails (d)
- two small pumpkins on stems (e)

tools and materials

- 5" (12.7 cm) cube vase
- 3" (7.6 cm) cube vase
- candy corn or other filler material
- floral tape or clear anchor tape
- ½ yd. (0.5 m) ribbon
- 6" (15.2 cm) wired wood pick
- scissors
- wire cutter

1 Wash and dry the vases. Set the smaller vase into the center of the larger vase.

2 Fill the space between vases with candy corn or other colorful, interesting material.

3   Cut all the flower and pumpkin stems to 9" (22.9 cm). Form them into a small hand-tied bouquet. Add the cattails into the center so they rise above the flowers. Wrap the bouquet with floral tape.

4   Place the bouquet into the center vase, allowing it to rest over the rim of the vase.

5   Make a small bow with the ribbon, tying it with the wire of the wood pick. Insert the pick into the side of the design.

6   Look over the design and make any necessary adjustments.

design tip

Change the filler to match the season: use candy hearts for Valentine's Day, pastel candies for Easter, peppermint pinwheels for Christmas, dried cranberries for Thanksgiving. Put water in the center vase and float fresh flower blossoms or a floating candle.

december fireworks

Casual garden-style arrangements are easy to put together and can be very impressive. The way these flowers burst upward from the container and then fall in graceful arcs toward the base reminds me of fireworks. A beaded garland drapes around the neck of the vase and falls to the table like a trail of sparks, adding festive flair. The large glass ginger jar used for this design has subtle striped texture that magnifies and distorts the stems, so imperfections and short ends won't matter.

florals

- one bush of larkspur with six stems
- six stems peony (a)
- four stems white lilies, each with two blossoms and a bud (b)
- four stems larkspur (c)
- three stipa berry branches (d)
- one berry bush with six stems (e)
- three stems cymbidium orchids (f)

tools and materials

- clear glass ginger jar vase, 13" (33 cm) tall with 6" (15.2 cm) rim
- 4 cups clear and red glass marbles
- bead garland
- scissors
- wire cutter

1 Wash and dry the vase. Gently place stones or marbles in the bottom of the vase for visual weight and stability.

2 Cut each bush into individual stems, keeping stems 8" (20.3 cm) or longer. Remove foliage from all the stems. Cut off any plastic pegs that held foliage. Set the stems aside in groups.

3

4

3 Cut 3" (7.6 cm) from the bottom of one peony stem, 2" (5 cm) from the bottom of one stem, 1" (2.5 cm) from the bottom of two stems, and leave the remaining two stems full length. Insert the peonies into the vase at 12:00, 2:00, 4:00, 6:00, 8:00, and 10:00, alternating from side to side and crisscrossing the stems in the vase. Place the taller stems closer to the center and shorter stems closer to the outside; turn their faces outward and upward.

4 Cut 2" (5 cm) from the bottom of two lily stems. Insert the lilies evenly spaced among the peonies.

5 Cut 2" (5 cm) from the bottom of two larkspur stems. Insert the larkspur stems evenly spaced throughout the arrangement. Add the stems cut from the larkspur bush.

5

6

6 Add the orchid stems draping down and out so they are easily visible.

7 Insert the berry stems in clusters, longer stems higher in the arrangement, shorter stems closer to the lip around the bottom. Have the berries drape out and down.

8 Wrap the bead garland around the neck of the vase. Join the ends and let the tails drape down the side of the vase onto the table.

9 Look over the design and make any necessary adjustments.

8

fresh idea

Try fresh flowers in this design, and use fresh water with flower food. Using a sharp knife or oriental shears, cut the stems at an angle at various lengths and insert them in the same order as for the faux arrangement. If peonies are hard to find, substitute open roses. For accent, add red berry stems and long-needle pine or cedar boughs.

about the *author*

Photo: John S. Macienjy

Ardith Beveridge, AIFD, AAF, PFCI, is a master floral designer, educator, and judge. She is the director of education and instructor for the Koehler & Dramm Institute of Floristry. She also co-owns a floral design video production company, Floral Communications Group, Inc., and is the instructor in the company's twelve series of do-it-yourself videos. Ardith's creativity and enthusiasm have captivated audiences in programs and workshops across the country and internationally. Ardith has designed for presidential inaugurations and other prestigious national and international events. She also appears regularly on television. She is a design education specialist for Teleflora wire service, a Smithers Oasis design director, and a master designer for FTD. In 2005, Ardith was inducted into the South Dakota Florist's Association Hall of Fame.

index

CPSIA information can be obtained at www.ICGtesting.com
Printed in the USA
LVOW02s1908110714

393960LV00004B/5/P